3 INGREDIENTS
DIABETES
COOKBOOK

Simple, Flavorful & Healthy 3 Ingredients
Dishes for Diabetes

Anna Roberts

CONTENTS

3 INGREDIENTS

Mediterranean Quinoa Salad
Eggplant And Tomato Bake
Lentil And Vegetable Stew
Brussels Sprouts And Walnut Salad
Zucchini Noodles With Pesto

CHAPTER SIX
SOUPS & SARNIES

Minestrone Soup With Turkey Sandwich
Lentil Soup With Chicken Salad Wrap
Tomato Basil Soup With Caprese Panini
Vegetable Noodle Soup With Turkey And Avocado Wrap
Mushroom Barley Soup With Tuna Salad Pita
Broccoli Cheddar Soup With Turkey And Cranberry Sandwich

CHICKEN AND RICE SOUP WITH HUMMUS VEGGIE WRAP
Sweet Potato And Carrot Soup With Turkey And Apple Panini
Quinoa And Vegetable Soup With Hummus And Veggie Wrap
Spinach And Mushroom Soup With Turkey And Avocado Roll

3 INGREDIENTS

PREFACE

The doctor's words hung heavy in the air: "**pre-diabetic**." Denial morphed into fear, then a flicker of defiance ignited within me. This wasn't a sentence; it was a challenge. I wouldn't succumb to bland restrictions; I would rewrite my health story with flavor and flair. My pantry resembled a war zone – a fortress of sugary treats and tempting processed foods. I knew change was necessary, but the thought of complex recipes and endless meal planning was daunting. That's when the magic of three ingredients emerged.

It started simple. A sprinkle of herbs transformed grilled chicken into a symphony of taste. A drizzle of balsamic vinegar elevated roasted vegetables to gourmet heights. Each discovery fueled my culinary exploration. Restaurant-worthy salmon with just honey mustard and lemon juice? Delicious. Creamy avocado pasta with a touch of garlic? Divine.

This journey wasn't just about food. It was about reclaiming my health and discovering a vibrant community. Online forums offered camaraderie and inspiration, while conversations with fellow "glucose warriors" fueled my spirit. Laughter echoed in kitchens filled with the satisfying sizzle of air fryers and the comforting aroma of slow-cooked meals.

This book, "**3 Ingredients Diabetics Cookbook**," is a testament to that transformation. It's more than just a collection of recipes; it's a battle cry for anyone facing similar challenges. Within these pages, you'll find:

- Delicious, Easy-To-Follow 3 Ingredients Recipes

Each dish requires just three core ingredients, making them perfect for busy schedules and limited cooking experience.

- Hidden Health Benefits

Every recipe is strategically crafted to manage blood sugar levels, incorporating protein, fiber, and healthy fats for balanced nutrition.

- Portion Control

Effective diabetes management relies heavily on portion control. We understand the value of balanced servings and offer clear, practical instructions to help you approach each meal mindfully.

- Confidently Count Carbohydrates

Knowledge is power, particularly when it comes to carbohydrates. We provide thorough carbohydrate content statistics for each recipe, allowing you to make informed decisions about your daily intake while maintaining stable blood sugar levels.

- Wholesome Ingredients for Wholehearted Cooking

Our culinary concept emphasizes the simplicity and purity of natural, unadulterated ingredients.

3 INGREDIENTS

Fresh fruits, vegetables, lean proteins, and whole grains take center stage, ensuring that your culinary creations provide a nourishing experience.

- Practical advice and Tactics

This book will assist you in creating well-balanced, diabetes-friendly meals that are tailored to your taste   preferences.

Are you ready to embark on this culinary adventure? **Let's Go!**

CHAPTER ONE
COOKING MADE EASY, ENJOYABLE & NUTRITIOUS

Cooking should be a fun and accessible pastime for anybody, regardless of expertise level. The "**3 Ingredients Diabetics Cookbook**" aims to make the kitchen a source of inspiration and empowerment. From the inexperienced cook looking for simplicity to the seasoned chef looking for quick and nutritious options, these recipes are designed with accessibility in mind, making creating a diabetes-friendly dinner both pleasant and stress-free.

Before you begin reading these recipes, take a moment to familiarize yourself with the cookbook's structure. Each chapter focuses on a single mealtime or type of cuisine, offering a full guidance to breakfast, lunch, supper, sweets, and snacks.

Each dish includes clear instructions and bright graphics to stimulate your senses.

LIFESTYLE

The "3 Ingredients Diabetics Cookbook" is more than simply a collection of recipes; it's a tool to assist you on your path to a healthy lifestyle. This cookbook contains recommendations on item substitutions, portion control, and eating a balanced diet. By adopting these habits into your daily routine, you will not only efficiently control diabetes but also improve your general well-being.

TAKING A MINDFUL WHOLESOME APPROACH

The "3 Ingredients Diabetics Cookbook" is a concept that engages conscious eating is essential for a healthier living. It encourages you to relish each bite, appreciate the flavors, and enjoy the nutrients that comes with a well-balanced meal. Fostering a conscious and healthful approach to cooking and eating not only benefits your physical health but also helps you develop a positive relationship with food.

SUSTAINABILITY IN THE KITCHEN

As we work through the dishes, let us evaluate the environmental impact of our culinary choices. The **"3 Ingredients Diabetics Cookbook"** promotes sustainable practices such as using locally obtained ingredients, reducing food waste, and looking into plant-based alternatives. Small changes in our culinary practices can help to create a healthier planet, which aligns with our dedication to total well-being.

The journey does not finish with the final recipe in this book. This cookbook can serve as a starting point for further culinary discovery. Experiment with new ingredients, different culinary methods, and broaden your repertoire.

The skills you gain from these pages will not only improve your ability to prepare excellent meals, but will also enable you to make educated decisions outside of the scope of this cookbook.

In the hustle and bustle of daily life, we frequently forget the simple joys that come from making and eating a delicious meal.

The "**3 Ingredients Diabetics Cookbook**" invites you to calm down, savor the cooking process, and enjoy the satisfaction of nourishing your body with nutritious ingredients. By including these little joys into your daily routine, you may elevate the act of eating to a celebration of health and wellness.

Each carefully designed recipe is more than just a

collection of ingredients; it is a step toward improved health, enhanced energy and most importantly, a more vibrant life.

Beyond the Plate

While this cookbook focuses on the nutritional components of diabetes management, we understand that overall wellbeing goes beyond the plate. Throughout these pages, you'll find tips for incorporating physical activity, mindfulness practices, and stress management into your everyday routine.

The holistic approach to wellness promotes a balanced lifestyle that extends beyond what is on your plate, with the goal of improving your health. We invite you to try the many culinary experiences given here and see how varied flavors can be tastefully merged into a diabetes-friendly lifestyle.

As you turn the pages and explore the recipes in the "**3 Ingredients Diabetics Cookbook**," keep in mind that you're doing more than simply cooking; you're also building a connection with your health, your loved ones, and a community of others who are on the same journey.

Allow the delight of cooking, the pleasure of sharing meals, and the celebration of health to be your continuous friends.

Enjoy!

Berry Bliss Bowl

Ingredients

- 1 cup mixed berries (strawberries, blueberries, raspberries)
- 1 medium banana, sliced
- 1/2 cup Greek yogurt (unsweetened)

1 tablespoon chia seeds (Optional)

Instructions

1. In a bowl, combine the mixed berries and sliced banana.
2. Add the Greek yogurt to the bowl.
3. Sprinkle chia seeds over the mixture.
4. If desired, drizzle honey or maple syrup for added sweetness.
5. Gently mix all the ingredients until well combined.
6. Allow the bowl to sit for a few minutes to let the chia seeds absorb some liquid and thicken the yogurt.
7. Top the bowl with granola for added crunch and texture.

Nutritional Value (per serving)

- Calories: 250 kcal
- Protein: 10g
- Carbohydrates: 45g
- Dietary Fiber: 8g
- Sugars: 25g
- Fat: 5g
- Saturated Fat: 1g

3 INGREDIENTS

- Cholesterol: 5mg
- Sodium: 30mg
- Potassium: 500mg

Number of Servings: 2

Avocado & Tomato Salad

Ingredients

- Avocado
- Cherry tomatoes
- Olive oil

Instructions

1. Slice the avocado and halve the cherry tomatoes.
2. Combine the sliced avocado and halved cherry tomatoes in a bowl.
3. Drizzle with olive oil and gently toss to coat.
4. Serve immediately and enjoy this refreshing salad!

Nutritional Value (per serving)

- Calories: 180
- Total Fat: 15g
- Carbohydrates: 10g
- Fiber: 7g
- Protein: 2g

Number of Servings: 2

Grilled Salmon with Lemon

Ingredients

- Salmon fillet
- Lemon
- Dill (optional)

Instructions

1. Preheat the grill or oven.
2. Place the salmon fillet on a piece of foil.
3. Squeeze lemon juice over the salmon and add dill if desired.
4. Grill or bake until the salmon is cooked through.
5. Serve with additional lemon wedges if desired.

Nutritional Value (per serving):

- Calories: 250
- Total Fat: 14g
- Carbohydrates: 1g
- Fiber: 0g
- Protein: 30g

Number of Servings: 1

Greek Yogurt Parfait

Ingredients

- Greek yogurt (unsweetened)
- Berries (strawberries, blueberries, or raspberries)
- Almonds (chopped)

Instructions

1. In a glass or bowl, layer Greek yogurt at the bottom.

2. Add a layer of fresh berries on top.
3. Sprinkle chopped almonds over the berries.
4. Repeat the layers until you reach the top.
5. Serve immediately for a delicious and nutritious parfait.

Nutritional Value (per serving)

- Calories: 220
- Total Fat: 12g
- Carbohydrates: 15g
- Fiber: 5g
- Protein: 15g

Number of Servings: 1

CHAPTER TWO
3 INGREDIENTS BREAKFAST RECIPES

Almond Butter Banana Toast

Ingredients

- 1 slice whole-grain bread
- 1 tablespoon almond butter
- 1/2 banana, sliced

Instructions

1. Toast the whole-grain bread.
2. Spread almond butter evenly on the toast.
3. Top with banana slices.
4. A quick and satisfying breakfast is ready!

Nutritional Value (per serving)

- Calories: 250

- Total Fat: 11g

- Carbohydrates: 32g

- Fiber: 6g

- Protein: 7g

Number of Servings: 1

Greek Yogurt with Walnuts

Ingredients

- 1 cup plain Greek yogurt (unsweetened)
- 1/4 cup walnuts, chopped
- 1 tablespoon honey (optional)

Instructions

1. Spoon Greek yogurt into a bowl.
2. Sprinkle chopped walnuts on top.
3. Drizzle with honey if desired.
4. A protein-packed breakfast is served!

Nutritional Value (per serving)

- Calories: 280

- Total Fat: 18g

- Carbohydrates: 16g

- Fiber: 2g

- Protein: 18g

Number of Servings: 1

Egg and Spinach Wrap

Ingredients

- 2 large eggs
- Handful of fresh spinach
- 1 whole-grain tortilla

Instructions

1. Scramble the eggs in a pan until cooked.
2. Add fresh spinach to the pan and cook until wilted.

3. Place the egg and spinach mixture in a whole-grain tortilla. Roll it up and enjoy!

Nutritional Value (per serving)

- Calories: 320

- Total Fat: 16g

- Carbohydrates: 22g

- Fiber: 6g

- Protein: 22g

Number of Servings: 1

Cottage Cheese with Pineapple

Ingredients

- 1/2 cup low-fat cottage cheese
- 1/2 cup fresh pineapple chunks
- 1 tablespoon flaxseeds (optional)

Instructions

1. Combine cottage cheese and pineapple in a bowl.

2. Sprinkle flaxseeds on top if desired.

3. A quick and satisfying protein-rich breakfast!

Nutritional Value (per serving)

- Calories: 180

- Total Fat: 4g

- Carbohydrates: 24g

- Fiber: 3g

- Protein: 15g

Number of Servings: 1

Chia Seed Pudding

Ingredients

- 2 tablespoons chia seeds
- 1/2 cup unsweetened almond milk
- 1/4 cup fresh berries

Instructions

1. Mix chia seeds and almond milk in a bowl.
2. Let it sit in the refrigerator for at least 2 hours or overnight.

3. Top with fresh berries before serving.
4. A delicious and fiber-rich pudding is ready!

Nutritional Value (per serving)

- Calories: 150

- Total Fat: 8g

- Carbohydrates: 15g

- Fiber: 10g

- Protein: 5g

Number of Servings: 1

Peanut Butter Banana Smoothie

Ingredients

- 1 banana
- 2 tablespoons peanut butter (unsweetened)
- 1 cup unsweetened almond milk

Instructions

1. Blend banana, peanut butter, and almond milk until smooth.

2. Pour into a glass and enjoy this protein-packed smoothie.

Nutritional Value (per serving)

- Calories: 280

- Total Fat: 18g

- Carbohydrates: 25g

- Fiber: 5g

- Protein: 9g

Number of Servings: 1

Yogurt Parfait with Berries

Ingredients

1. 1 cup plain yogurt (unsweetened)
2. 1/2 cup mixed berries (strawberries, blueberries)
3. 1/4 cup granola (low-sugar)

Instructions

1. Layer yogurt, berries, and granola in a glass or bowl.
2. Repeat the layers until the ingredients are used.
3. A tasty and satisfying parfait is ready to be enjoyed!

Nutritional Value (per serving)

- Calories: 230

- Total Fat: 8g

- Carbohydrates: 30g

- Fiber: 4g

- Protein: 12g

Number of Servings: 1

Turkey and Cheese Roll-Ups

Ingredients

- 4 slices turkey breast
- 2 slices Swiss cheese
- 1/2 avocado, sliced

Instructions

1. Place a slice of Swiss cheese on each turkey slice.
2. Add avocado slices on top.

3. Roll up and secure with toothpicks if needed.
4. A protein-rich, low-carb breakfast is served!

Nutritional Value (per serving)

- Calories: 220

- Total Fat: 15g

- Carbohydrates: 4g

- Fiber: 3g

- Protein: 18g

Number of Servings: 1

Chocolate Banana Smoothie Bowl

Ingredients

1. 1 banana
2. 2 tablespoons unsweetened cocoa powder
3. 1/2 cup unsweetened almond milk

Instructions

1. Blend banana, cocoa powder, and almond milk until smooth.

2. Pour into a bowl and add your favorite toppings.
3. A chocolatey and satisfying breakfast treat!

Nutritional Value (per serving)

- Calories: 200

- Total Fat: 10g

- Carbohydrates: 30g

- Fiber: 8g

- Protein: 5g

Number of Servings: 1

CHAPTER THREE
BUDGET FRIENDLY LUNCH RECIPES

Quinoa and Vegetable Stir-Fry

Ingredients

- Quinoa
- Mixed vegetables (bell peppers, broccoli, carrots)
- Low-sodium soy sauce

Instructions

1. Cook quinoa according to package instructions.
2. Stir-fry mixed vegetables in a pan with a small amount of oil.
3. Add cooked quinoa and soy sauce, toss until well combined.
4. Serve warm.

Nutritional Value (per serving)

- Calories: 250

- Total Fat: 5g

- Carbohydrates: 45g

- Fiber: 7g

- Protein: 8g

Number of Servings: 4

Turkey and Black Bean Lettuce Wraps

Ingredients

- Ground turkey
- Black beans (canned, rinsed)
- Lettuce leaves

Instructions

1. Brown ground turkey in a pan.
2. Add black beans and cook until heated through.

3. Spoon the mixture into lettuce leaves.
4. Roll and secure with toothpicks.
5. Serve with your favorite salsa or Greek yogurt.

Nutritional Value (per serving)

- Calories: 280

- Total Fat: 10g

- Carbohydrates: 20g

- Fiber: 6g

- Protein: 25g

Number of Servings: 3

INGREDIENTS

Egg and Vegetable Skillet

Ingredients

- Eggs
- Spinach
- Cherry tomatoes

Instructions

1. In a skillet, sauté spinach until wilted.
2. Crack eggs over the spinach, add cherry tomatoes.
3. Scramble until eggs are cooked.
4. Season with salt and pepper.

51

5. Serve hot.

Nutritional Value (per serving)

- Calories: 200

- Total Fat: 12g

- Carbohydrates: 8g

- Fiber: 3g

- Protein: 15g

Number of Servings: 2

Chickpea Salad

Ingredients

- Canned chickpeas (rinsed)
- Cucumber
- Feta cheese (optional)

Instructions

1. Mix chickpeas and chopped cucumber in a bowl.

2. Add crumbled feta cheese if desired.
3. Drizzle with olive oil and toss.
4. Season with salt and pepper.
5. Serve chilled.

Nutritional Value (per serving)

- Calories: 220

- Total Fat: 8g

- Carbohydrates: 30g

- Fiber: 8g

- Protein: 10g

Number of Servings: 3

Tomato Basil Mozzarella Salad

Ingredients

- Cherry tomatoes
- Fresh mozzarella
- Fresh basil leaves

Instructions

1. Slice cherry tomatoes and mozzarella.
2. Arrange on a plate with fresh basil leaves.
3. Drizzle with balsamic glaze or olive oil.

4. Sprinkle with salt and pepper.
5. Serve as a refreshing salad.

Nutritional Value (per serving)

- Calories: 180

- Total Fat: 12g

- Carbohydrates: 5g

- Fiber: 1g

- Protein: 14g

Number of Servings: 2

Mushroom and Spinach Quesadillas

Ingredients

1. Whole wheat tortillas

2. Mushrooms

3. Spinach

Instructions

1. Sauté mushrooms and spinach in a pan until cooked.
2. Place the mixture on a tortilla.
3. Top with another tortilla and press down.

4. Cook on both sides until golden.
5. Slice into wedges and serve.

Nutritional Value (per serving)

- Calories: 220

- Total Fat: 8g

- Carbohydrates: 30g

- Fiber: 6g

- Protein: 10g

Number of Servings: 2

Lentil Soup

Ingredients

- Dry lentils
- Carrots
- Low-sodium vegetable broth

Instructions

1. Rinse lentils and cook in vegetable broth.
2. Add diced carrots and simmer until lentils are tender.

3. Season with herbs and spices of choice.
4. Serve hot.

Nutritional Value (per serving)

- Calories: 180

- Total Fat: 1g

- Carbohydrates: 30g

- Fiber: 12g

- Protein: 13g

Number of Servings: 4

Sweet Potato and Chickpea Curry

Ingredients

- Sweet potatoes
- Canned chickpeas (rinsed)
- Curry powder

Instructions

1. Dice sweet potatoes and boil until tender.

2. In a pan, combine chickpeas, sweet potatoes, and curry powder.
3. Simmer until heated through.
4. Serve over brown rice or quinoa.

Nutritional Value (per serving)

- Calories: 250

- Total Fat: 2g

- Carbohydrates: 50g

- Fiber: 10g

- Protein: 8g

Number of Servings: 3

Tuna and White Bean Salad

Ingredients

- Canned tuna (in water)
- White beans (canned, rinsed)
- Red onion

Instructions

1. Mix tuna, white beans, and diced red onion in a bowl.
2. Drizzle with olive oil and toss.
3. Season with salt and pepper.

4. Serve as a protein-packed salad.

Nutritional Value (per serving)

- Calories: 230

- Total Fat: 5g

- Carbohydrates: 25g

- Fiber: 6g

- Protein: 20g

Number of Servings: 2

Vegetarian Chili

Ingredients

- Black beans (canned, rinsed)
- Diced tomatoes (canned)
- Chili powder

Instructions

1. Combine black beans and diced tomatoes in a pot.

2. Stir in chili powder and simmer until flavors meld.
3. Serve hot with a dollop of Greek yogurt.

Nutritional Value (per serving)

- Calories: 200

- Total Fat: 2g

- Carbohydrates: 40g

- Fiber: 14g

- Protein: 10g

Number of Servings: 4

CHAPTER FOUR
3 INGREDIENTS SEAFOODS & FISH MEALS

Baked Lemon Herb Salmon

Ingredients

- Salmon fillet
- Fresh lemon
- Dill (fresh or dried)

Instructions

1. Preheat the oven to 375°F (190°C).
2. Place the salmon fillet on a baking sheet.
3. Squeeze fresh lemon juice over the salmon and sprinkle with dill.
4. Bake for 15-20 minutes or until the salmon flakes easily with a fork.
5. Serve with additional lemon wedges if desired.

Nutritional Value (per serving)

- Calories: 250

- Total Fat: 14g

- Carbohydrates: 1g

- Fiber: 0g

- Protein: 30g

Number of Servings: 2

Garlic Butter Shrimp

Ingredients

- Shrimp (peeled and deveined)
- Butter
- Garlic (minced)

Instructions

1. In a skillet, melt butter over medium heat.
2. Add minced garlic and cook until fragrant.

3. Add shrimp and cook until they turn pink and opaque.
4. Serve the garlic butter shrimp over a bed of steamed vegetables or cauliflower rice.

Nutritional Value (per serving)

- Calories: 180

- Total Fat: 10g

- Carbohydrates: 2g

- Fiber: 0g

- Protein: 20g

Number of Servings: 2

Lemon Garlic Grilled Tilapia

Ingredients

- Tilapia fillet
- Fresh lemon
- Garlic powder

Instructions

1. Preheat the grill or stovetop grill pan.
2. Place the tilapia fillet on the grill.
3. Squeeze fresh lemon juice over the tilapia and sprinkle with garlic powder.

4. Grill for 3-4 minutes per side or until the fish is cooked through.
5. Serve with a wedge of lemon.

Nutritional Value (per serving)

- Calories: 150

- Total Fat: 3g

- Carbohydrates: 2g

- Fiber: 0g

- Protein: 30g

Number of Servings: 2

Cajun Baked Catfish

Ingredients

- Catfish fillet
- Cajun seasoning
- Olive oil

Instructions

1. Preheat the oven to 375°F (190°C).
2. Place the catfish fillet on a baking sheet.
3. Drizzle with olive oil and sprinkle generously with Cajun seasoning.

4. Bake for 20-25 minutes or until the catfish flakes easily.
5. Serve with a side of sautéed spinach or steamed vegetables.

Nutritional Value (per serving)

- Calories: 200

- Total Fat: 10g

- Carbohydrates: 1g

- Fiber: 0g

- Protein: 25g

Number of Servings: 2

Lemon Dijon Grilled Shrimp

Ingredients

- Shrimp (peeled and deveined)
- Dijon mustard
- Fresh lemon

Instructions

1. In a bowl, mix Dijon mustard with fresh lemon juice.

2. Marinate the shrimp in the mixture for 15-20 minutes.
3. Thread shrimp onto skewers and grill for 2-3 minutes per side.
4. Serve with additional lemon wedges.

Nutritional Value (per serving)

- Calories: 160

- Total Fat: 5g

- Carbohydrates: 2g

- Fiber: 0g

- Protein: 25g

Number of Servings: 2

Sesame Ginger Baked Cod

Ingredients

- Cod fillet
- Soy sauce (low-sodium)
- Sesame seeds

Instructions

1. Preheat the oven to 375°F (190°C).
2. Place the cod fillet on a baking sheet.

3. Brush with soy sauce and sprinkle with sesame seeds.
4. Bake for 15-20 minutes or until the cod is cooked through.
5. Serve over a bed of steamed broccoli or cauliflower rice.

Nutritional Value (per serving)

- Calories: 180

- Total Fat: 5g

- Carbohydrates: 2g

- Fiber: 0g

- Protein: 30g

Number of Servings: 2

Mustard Glazed Salmon

Ingredients

- Salmon fillet
- Dijon mustard
- Honey

Instructions

1. Preheat the oven to 375°F (190°C).
2. Mix Dijon mustard with honey to create a glaze.

3. Brush the glaze over the salmon fillet.
4. Bake for 15-20 minutes or until the salmon is cooked through.
5. Serve with a side of steamed asparagus or green beans.

Nutritional Value (per serving)

- Calories: 220

- Total Fat: 12g

- Carbohydrates: 5g

- Fiber: 0g

- Protein: 25g

Number of Servings: 2

Pesto Baked Haddock

Ingredients

- Haddock fillet
- Pesto sauce
- Cherry tomatoes (optional)

Instructions

1. Preheat the oven to 375°F (190°C).
2. Place the haddock fillet on a baking sheet.
3. Spread pesto sauce over the haddock.
4. Add cherry tomatoes on top (optional).

5. Bake for 15-20 minutes or until the haddock is cooked through.
6. Serve with a squeeze of fresh lemon.

Nutritional Value (per serving)

- Calories: 190

- Total Fat: 10g

- Carbohydrates: 3g

- Fiber: 1g

- Protein: 25g

Number of Servings: 2

Lemon Pepper Grilled Shrimp Skewers

Ingredients

- Shrimp (peeled and deveined)
- Fresh lemon
- Black pepper

Instructions

1. Preheat the grill.
2. Thread shrimp onto skewers.

3. Squeeze fresh lemon juice over the shrimp and sprinkle with black pepper.
4. Grill for 2-3 minutes per side or until the shrimp are pink and opaque.
5. Serve with a side of mixed greens or a green salad.

Nutritional Value (per serving)

- Calories: 160

- Total Fat: 3g

- Carbohydrates: 2g

- Fiber: 0g

- Protein: 30g

Number of Servings: 2

Chili Lime Baked Red Snapper

Ingredients

- Red snapper fillet
- Chili powder
- Fresh lime

Instructions

1. Preheat the oven to 375°F (190°C).
2. Place the red snapper fillet on a baking sheet.
3. Sprinkle chili powder over the fillet.

4. Squeeze fresh lime juice over the fish.
5. Bake for 15-20 minutes or until the red snapper is cooked through.
6. Serve with a side of sautéed spinach or quinoa.

Nutritional Value (per serving)

- Calories: 170

- Total Fat: 5g

- Carbohydrates: 3g

- Fiber: 1g

- Protein: 25g

Number of Servings: 2

CHAPTER FIVE
VEGETARIAN MEALS & SALADS

Quinoa and Roasted Vegetable Bowl

Ingredients

- Quinoa
- Mixed vegetables (zucchini, bell peppers, cherry tomatoes)
- Olive oil, salt, and pepper

Instructions

1. Cook quinoa according to package instructions.
2. Toss mixed vegetables in olive oil, salt, and pepper.
3. Roast vegetables until tender.
4. Serve roasted vegetables over cooked quinoa.

Nutritional Value (per serving)

- Calories: 300

- Total Fat: 10g

- Carbohydrates: 45g

- Fiber: 8g

- Protein: 10g

Number of Servings: 2

Chickpea and Spinach Salad

Ingredients

- Canned chickpeas (rinsed and drained)
- Fresh spinach
- Feta cheese, crumbled

Instructions

1. Combine chickpeas, fresh spinach, and crumbled feta in a bowl.
2. Toss gently to mix the ingredients.

3. Drizzle with olive oil and lemon juice if desired.

Nutritional Value (per serving)

- Calories: 250

- Total Fat: 12g

- Carbohydrates: 30g

- Fiber: 8g

- Protein: 12g

Number of Servings: 2

Cauliflower Fried Rice

Ingredients

- Cauliflower rice
- Mixed vegetables (peas, carrots, corn)
- Tofu, diced

Instructions

1. Sauté mixed vegetables and tofu in a pan.
2. Add cauliflower rice and stir-fry until cooked.
3. Season with low-sodium soy sauce.

Nutritional Value (per serving)

- Calories: 220

- Total Fat: 10g

- Carbohydrates: 25g

- Fiber: 8g

- Protein: 15g

Number of Servings 2

Caprese Salad

Ingredients

- Tomatoes
- Fresh mozzarella
- Fresh basil leaves

Instructions

1. Slice tomatoes and fresh mozzarella.
2. Arrange slices on a plate, alternating between tomatoes and mozzarella.

3. Tuck fresh basil leaves between the slices.

4. Drizzle with balsamic glaze.

Nutritional Value (per serving)

- Calories: 180

- Total Fat: 12g

- Carbohydrates: 6g

- Fiber: 2g

- Protein: 10g

Number of Servings: 2

Sweet Potato and Black Bean Bowl

Ingredients

- Sweet potatoes, cubed
- Black beans, canned and rinsed
- Avocado, sliced

Instructions

1. Roast sweet potato cubes until golden.

2. Mix with black beans and top with sliced avocado.

Nutritional Value (per serving)

- Calories: 280

- Total Fat: 10g

- Carbohydrates: 40g

- Fiber: 12g

- Protein: 10g

Number of Servings: 2

Mediterranean Quinoa Salad

Ingredients

- Quinoa
- Cucumber, diced
- Kalamata olives, sliced

Instructions

1. Cook quinoa according to package instructions.

2. Combine cooked quinoa with diced cucumber and sliced olives.
3. Drizzle with olive oil and lemon juice.

Nutritional Value (per serving)

- Calories: 260

- Total Fat: 12g

- Carbohydrates: 30g

- Fiber: 6g

- Protein: 8g

Number of Servings: 2

Eggplant and Tomato Bake

Ingredients

1. Eggplant, sliced
2. Tomatoes, sliced
3. Parmesan cheese, grated

Instructions

1. Layer sliced eggplant and tomatoes in a baking dish.
2. Sprinkle with grated Parmesan.
3. Bake until vegetables are tender.

Nutritional Value (per serving)

- Calories: 220

- Total Fat: 8g

- Carbohydrates: 30g

- Fiber: 10g

- Protein: 10g

Number of Servings: 2

Lentil and Vegetable Stew

Ingredients

- Lentils
- Mixed vegetables (carrots, celery, onion)
- Vegetable broth

Instructions

1. Sauté vegetables in a pot until softened.
2. Add lentils and vegetable broth.
3. Simmer until lentils are cooked through.

Nutritional Value (per serving)

- Calories: 240

- Total Fat: 2g

- Carbohydrates: 45g

- Fiber: 12g

- Protein: 15g

Number of Servings: 4

Brussels Sprouts and Walnut Salad

Ingredients

- Brussels sprouts, shaved
- Walnuts, chopped
- Pomegranate seeds

Instructions

1. Combine shaved Brussels sprouts, chopped walnuts, and pomegranate seeds.
2. Toss with a light vinaigrette.

Nutritional Value (per serving)

- Calories: 200

- Total Fat: 12g

- Carbohydrates: 18g

- Fiber: 7g

- Protein: 6g

Number of Servings: 2

Zucchini Noodles with Pesto

Ingredients

- Zucchini, spiralized
- Cherry tomatoes, halved
- Pesto sauce

Instructions

1. Spiralize zucchini into noodle shapes.
2. Toss zucchini noodles with halved cherry tomatoes.

3. Mix in pesto sauce and serve.

Nutritional Value (per serving)

- Calories: 180

- Total Fat: 14g

- Carbohydrates: 10g

- Fiber: 3g

- Protein: 5g

Number of Servings: 2

CHAPTER SIX
SOUPS & SARNIES

Minestrone Soup with Turkey Sandwich

Soup Ingredients

- Low-sodium vegetable broth
- Mixed vegetables (carrots, celery, zucchini)
- Canned diced tomatoes

Sandwich Ingredients

- Whole-grain bread
- Sliced turkey breast
- Spinach leaves

Instructions

1. In a pot, combine vegetable broth, mixed vegetables, and diced tomatoes. Simmer until vegetables are tender.
2. Toast whole-grain bread and layer with turkey and spinach to create a sandwich.
3. Serve the minestrone soup with the turkey sandwich.

Nutritional Value (per serving)

- Calories: 350

- Total Fat: 8g

- Carbohydrates: 45g

- Fiber: 10g

- Protein: 25g

Number of Servings: 2

Lentil Soup with Chicken Salad Wrap

Soup Ingredients

- Dried lentils
- Vegetable broth
- Onion and garlic

Sandwich Ingredients

- Grilled chicken breast

- Whole-grain wrap
- Greek yogurt-based dressing

Instructions

1. Cook lentils with vegetable broth, onion, and garlic until tender.
2. Shred grilled chicken and mix with Greek yogurt-based dressing. Fill the whole-grain wrap.
3. Serve lentil soup alongside the chicken salad wrap.

Nutritional Value (per serving)

- Calories: 380

- Total Fat: 9g

- Carbohydrates: 50g

- Fiber: 15g

- Protein: 30g

Number of Servings: 2

Tomato Basil Soup with Caprese Panini

Soup Ingredients

- Canned crushed tomatoes
- Fresh basil leaves
- Low-sodium vegetable broth

Sandwich Ingredients

- Whole-grain bread
- Mozzarella cheese
- Sliced tomatoes and fresh basil

Instructions

1. Simmer crushed tomatoes, fresh basil, and vegetable broth to make the tomato basil soup.
2. Assemble a Caprese Panini with whole-grain bread, mozzarella, sliced tomatoes, and fresh basil.
3. Serve the panini with a side of tomato basil soup.

Nutritional Value (per serving)

- Calories: 420

- Total Fat: 12g

- Carbohydrates: 55g

- Fiber: 12g

- Protein: 20g

Number of Servings: 2

Vegetable Noodle Soup with Turkey and Avocado Wrap

Soup Ingredients

- Low-sodium chicken or vegetable broth
- Mixed vegetables (carrots, peas, spinach)
- Whole-grain noodles

Sandwich Ingredients

- Sliced turkey breast
- Whole-grain wrap
- Sliced avocado

Instructions

1. Boil noodles in broth, add mixed vegetables, and cook until tender.
2. Create a turkey and avocado wrap with whole-grain bread.
3. Serve the vegetable noodle soup with the turkey and avocado wrap.

Nutritional Value (per serving)

- Calories: 380

- Total Fat: 10g

- Carbohydrates: 50g

- Fiber: 14g

- Protein: 25g

Number of Servings: 2

Mushroom Barley Soup with Tuna Salad Pita

Soup Ingredients

- Pearl barley
- Mushrooms
- Low-sodium beef or vegetable broth

Sandwich Ingredients

- Canned tuna
- Whole-grain pita

- Mixed greens and cherry tomatoes

Instructions

1. Cook barley and mushrooms in broth until fully cooked for the mushroom barley soup.
2. Mix canned tuna with mixed greens and cherry tomatoes. Fill a whole-grain pita.
3. Serve the mushroom barley soup with the tuna salad pita.

Nutritional Value (per serving)

- Calories: 350

- Total Fat: 8g

- Carbohydrates: 45g

- Fiber: 10g

- Protein: 20g

Number of Servings: 2

Broccoli Cheddar Soup with Turkey and Cranberry Sandwich

Soup Ingredients

- Fresh or frozen broccoli
- Low-sodium chicken or vegetable broth
- Sharp cheddar cheese

Sandwich Ingredients

1. Sliced turkey breast

2. Whole-grain bread

3. Cranberry sauce (no sugar added)

Instructions

1. Steam or boil broccoli, then blend with broth and cheddar cheese for the broccoli cheddar soup.
2. Create a turkey and cranberry sandwich with whole-grain bread.
3. Serve the soup with the turkey and cranberry sandwich.

Nutritional Value (per serving)

- Calories: 400

- Total Fat: 14g

- Carbohydrates: 50g

- Fiber: 9g

- Protein: 22g

Number of Servings: 2

Chicken and Rice Soup with Hummus Veggie Wrap

Soup Ingredients

- Cooked chicken breast
- Brown rice
- Low-sodium chicken broth

Sandwich Ingredients

- Whole-grain wrap
- Hummus
- Sliced cucumber, bell peppers, and cherry tomatoes

Instructions

1. Combine cooked chicken, brown rice, and chicken broth for the chicken and rice soup.
2. Spread hummus on a whole-grain wrap and fill with sliced cucumber, bell peppers, and cherry tomatoes.
3. Serve the soup with the hummus veggie wrap.

Nutritional Value (per serving)

- Calories: 380

- Total Fat: 10g

- Carbohydrates: 45g

- Fiber: 10g

- Protein: 28g

Number of Servings: 2

Sweet Potato and Carrot Soup with Turkey and Apple Panini

Soup Ingredients

- Sweet potatoes
- Carrots
- Low-sodium vegetable broth

Sandwich Ingredients

- Sliced turkey breast

- Whole-grain bread
- Sliced apple and cheddar cheese

Instructions

1. Boil sweet potatoes and carrots, then blend with vegetable broth for the sweet potato and carrot soup.
2. Assemble a panini with turkey, sliced apple, and cheddar cheese on whole-grain bread.
3. Serve the soup with the turkey and apple panini.

Nutritional Value (per serving)

- Calories: 420

- Total Fat: 12g

- Carbohydrates: 55g

- Fiber: 12g

- Protein: 22g

Number of Servings: 2

Quinoa and Vegetable Soup with Hummus and Veggie Wrap

Soup Ingredients

- Quinoa
- Mixed vegetables (broccoli, bell peppers, carrots)
- Low-sodium vegetable broth

Sandwich Ingredients

- Whole-grain wrap
- Hummus
- Sliced cucumber, tomato, and lettuce

Instructions

1. Cook quinoa and mixed vegetables in vegetable broth for the quinoa and vegetable soup.
2. Spread hummus on a whole-grain wrap and fill with sliced cucumber, tomato, and lettuce.
3. Serve the soup with the hummus and veggie wrap.

Nutritional Value (per serving)

- Calories: 380

- Total Fat: 10g

- Carbohydrates: 50g

- Fiber: 12g

- Protein: 20g

Number of Servings: 2

Spinach and Mushroom Soup with Turkey and Avocado Roll

Soup Ingredients

- Fresh spinach
- Mushrooms
- Low-sodium chicken or vegetable broth

Sandwich Ingredients

- Whole-grain roll
- Sliced turkey breast
- Sliced avocado

Instructions

1. Sauté spinach and mushrooms, then add to broth for the spinach and mushroom soup.
2. Create a sandwich with a whole-grain roll, sliced turkey, and avocado.
3. Serve the soup with the turkey and avocado roll.

Nutritional Value (per serving)

- Calories: 360

- Total Fat: 9g

- Carbohydrates: 45g

- Fiber: 10g

- Protein: 23g

Number of Servings: 2

CHAPTER SEVEN
MEAT, CHICKEN & DUCK RECIPES

Grilled Lemon Garlic Chicken

Ingredients

- Chicken breasts
- Garlic (minced)
- Lemon juice
- Olive oil

- Salt and pepper to taste

Instructions

1. In a bowl, mix minced garlic, lemon juice, olive oil, salt, and pepper.
2. Marinate chicken breasts in the mixture for at least 30 minutes.
3. Grill the chicken until cooked through.
4. Serve hot.

Nutritional Value (per serving)

- Calories: 200

- Total Fat: 10g

- Carbohydrates: 2g

- Fiber: 0g

- Protein: 25g

Number of Servings: 4

Zucchini Noodles with Turkey Bolognese

Ingredients

- Ground turkey
- Zucchini
- Sugar-free tomato sauce & Italian seasoning

Instructions

1. Brown ground turkey in a pan, add Italian seasoning.
2. Spiralize zucchini into noodles.

3. Add zucchini noodles and sugar-free tomato sauce to the pan.
4. Cook until zucchini is tender.
5. Serve with grated Parmesan if desired.

Nutritional Value (per serving)

- Calories: 180

- Total Fat: 8g

- Carbohydrates: 6g

- Fiber: 2g

- Protein: 20g

Number of Servings: 2

Baked Lemon Herb Salmon

Ingredients

- Salmon fillets
- Lemon zest
- Fresh herbs (rosemary, thyme) & Olive oil

Instructions

1. Preheat the oven and line a baking sheet with foil.

2. Place salmon fillets on the sheet.
3. Mix olive oil, lemon zest, and chopped herbs.
4. Brush the mixture over the salmon.
5. Bake until salmon flakes easily.

Nutritional Value (per serving)

- Calories: 220

- Total Fat: 12g

- Carbohydrates: 1g

- Fiber: 0g

- Protein: 25g

Number of Servings: 4

Stir-Fried Sesame Ginger Chicken

Ingredients

- Chicken thighs (sliced)
- Sesame oil
- Ginger (minced) & Soy sauce (low-sodium)

Instructions

1. Heat sesame oil in a wok or skillet.
2. Add sliced chicken and minced ginger, stir-fry until browned.

3. Pour in low-sodium soy sauce and cook until chicken is cooked through.
4. Serve over cauliflower rice or steamed broccoli.

Nutritional Value (per serving)

- Calories: 230

- Total Fat: 15g

- Carbohydrates: 3g

- Fiber: 1g

- Protein: 20g

Number of Servings: 3

Cilantro Lime Grilled Shrimp

Ingredients

- Shrimp (peeled and deveined)
- Fresh cilantro (chopped)
- Lime juice
- Olive oil

Instructions

1. Mix chopped cilantro, lime juice, and olive oil in a bowl.
2. Marinate shrimp in the mixture for 15-20 minutes.

3. Thread shrimp onto skewers and grill until opaque.
4. Serve with additional lime wedges.

Nutritional Value (per serving)

- Calories: 150

- Total Fat: 8g

- Carbohydrates: 1g

- Fiber: 0g

- Protein: 18g

Number of Servings: 4

Turkey and Spinach Stuffed Mushrooms

Ingredients

- Ground turkey
- Spinach (chopped)
- Mushrooms & Garlic (minced)

Instructions

1. Preheat the oven.
2. Brown ground turkey with minced garlic.
3. Mix in chopped spinach until wilted.
4. Stuff mushroom caps with the mixture.

5. Bake until mushrooms are tender.

Nutritional Value (per serving)

- Calories: 180

- Total Fat: 8g

- Carbohydrates: 4g

- Fiber: 2g

- Protein: 22g

Number of Servings: 4

Dijon Mustard Glazed Chicken Thighs

Ingredients

- Chicken thighs
- Dijon mustard
- Herbs de Provence

Instructions

1. Preheat the oven.
2. Mix Dijon mustard and Herbs de Provence in a bowl.

3. Coat chicken thighs with the mixture.
4. Bake until chicken is cooked through.

Nutritional Value (per serving)

- Calories: 210

- Total Fat: 12g

- Carbohydrates: 2g

- Fiber: 0g

- Protein: 24g

Number of Servings: 4

Garlic Rosemary Lamb Chops

Ingredients

- Lamb chops
- Garlic (minced)
- Fresh rosemary (chopped)

Instructions

1. Preheat the grill or oven.
2. Rub lamb chops with minced garlic and chopped rosemary.
3. Grill or bake until lamb is cooked to desired doneness.
4. Let rest before serving.

Nutritional Value (per serving)

- Calories: 240

- Total Fat: 15g

- Carbohydrates: 0g

- Fiber: 0g

- Protein: 26g

Number of Servings: 2

Orange Glazed Duck Breast

Ingredients

- Duck breasts
- Orange zest and juice
- Low-sodium soy sauce

Instructions

1. Score duck breast skin and season with salt.
2. In a bowl, mix orange zest, juice, and soy sauce.
3. Brush the mixture over duck breasts.
4. Roast in the oven until the skin is crispy and duck is cooked.

5. Let rest before slicing.

Nutritional Value (per serving)

- Calories: 280

- Total Fat: 20g

- Carbohydrates: 3g

- Fiber: 1g

- Protein: 22g

Number of Servings: 2

CHAPTER EIGHT
THE 7-DAY ULTIMATE MEAL PLAN

- Day 1

Breakfast: Scrambled Eggs with Spinach and Whole Grain Toast

Lunch: Grilled Chicken Salad with Mixed Greens, Cherry Tomatoes, and Olive Oil Dressing

Dinner: Baked Salmon with Lemon, Quinoa, and Steamed Broccoli

Snack: Greek Yogurt with a Handful of Almonds

- Day 2

Breakfast: Overnight Oats with Berries and Chia Seeds

Lunch: Turkey and Avocado Wrap with Whole Wheat Tortilla

Dinner: Stir-Fried Tofu with Vegetables and Brown Rice

Snack: Carrot Sticks with Hummus

- Day 3

Breakfast: Smoothie Bowl with Mixed Berries, Greek Yogurt, and Almond Butter

Lunch: Quinoa Salad with Chickpeas, Cucumber, and Feta Cheese

Dinner: Grilled Shrimp Skewers with Asparagus and Quinoa

Snack: Apple Slices with Peanut Butter

- Day 4

Breakfast: Whole Grain Pancakes with Sugar-Free Syrup and Fresh Strawberries

Lunch: Lentil Soup with a Side of Mixed Greens

Dinner: Baked Chicken Breast with Sweet Potato Wedges and Green Beans

Snack: Cottage Cheese with Pineapple Chunks

- Day 5

Breakfast: Veggie Omelette with Tomatoes, Spinach, and Mushrooms

Lunch: Spinach and Feta Stuffed Bell Peppers with a Side Salad

Dinner: Beef Stir-Fry with Broccoli and Cauliflower Rice

Snack: Handful of Walnuts and a Small Orange

- Day 6

Breakfast: Whole Grain Toast with Smashed Avocado and Poached Egg

Lunch: Salmon Salad with Avocado, Quinoa, and Balsamic Vinaigrette

Dinner: Turkey and Vegetable Kebabs with Bulgur

Snack: Celery Sticks with Cream Cheese

- Day 7

Breakfast: Cottage Cheese and Pineapple Smoothie

Lunch: Caprese Salad with Grilled Chicken Breast

Dinner: Baked Cod with Lemon-Dill Sauce, Brown Rice, and Steamed Asparagus

Snack: Mixed Berries with a Dollop of Greek Yogurt

RECIPES CHECKLIST

A recipe checklist can help you stay organized, efficient, and avoid mistakes in the kitchen. It saves time, allows for ingredient replacements, and is flexible to individual preferences.

It makes purchasing easier, assures consistency, and works as a teaching tool. Ultimately, it minimizes tension, resulting in a more joyful culinary experience.

WHAT YOU NEED TO KNOW

- Stay hydrated by drinking plenty of water throughout the day.

- Portion control is essential; be mindful of serving sizes.

- Monitor blood sugar levels regularly and adjust the meal plan as needed.

- Include a variety of colorful vegetables to ensure a range of nutrients.

- Consider consulting with a healthcare professional or dietitian for personalized advice.

Dear Valued Reader,

I hope you enjoyed my book. I poured my heart and soul into it, and I'm so grateful that you took the time to read it.

If you found the book helpful, insightful, or entertaining, I would be honored if you would consider leaving a positive review.

Your feedback means the world to me as an author, and it can help other potential readers discover my work.

Thank you very much, God bless your kind heart.

Made in the USA
Columbia, SC
21 November 2024